Birds, Bees and Butterflies

ABCs

How They Help Our Food to Grow

by Heather Conrad

Lightport Books
Celebrating Biodiversity

In acknowledgment of the wise advice and assistance given by Kate Colwell, Mary Foley, Ginny Orenstein and Sandra Treacy—many thanks!

Copyright © Lightport Books 2016
Published in the United States by Lightport Books
P.O. Box 7112, Berkeley, CA 94707
All rights reserved.

ISBN 978-0-9712425-4-8

Picture Credits
The publisher would like to thank the following for permission to reproduce their material. Every care has been taken to accurately credit copyright holders. However, if there is an unintentional error, we apologize and will, if informed, correct it in any future edition.
Page R, Red Admiral: Charles J Sharp of Sharp Photography, posted on Wikimedia Commons 6/29/14 under the Creative Commons Attribution-Share Alike 4.0 International license. It has been cropped for this book.
Page X, Xerces blue: Brianwray 26, posted on Wikimedia Commons 10/28/12 under the Creative Commons Attribution-Share Alike 4.0 International license. It has been cropped for this book.
Page "How They Help Our Food to Grow, Eating Bugs", Olive-backed Pippit: Alpsdake, posted on Wikimedia Commons 2/7/14 under the Creative Commons Attribution-Share Alike 3.0 Unported. It has been cropped for this book.
Page C, Cedar waxwing and Checkerspot, and Page I, Ibis: Kate Colwell
All other photographs in this book: Heather Conrad

Reference
The Natural Resources Defense Council (www.nrdc.org), "BeeFacts", March 2011, provides information about the process of cross-pollination and how it helps over 30% of the world's crops and 90% of wild plants to thrive.
This book was inspired by the "Bring Back the Pollinators" campaign and the important work of The Xerces Society (www.xerces.org).

Introduction

This is an ABC book about birds, bees and butterflies around the world. In this book, you can look at pictures of these beautiful creatures and learn their names while also learning the alphabet. You can also try to find some of the birds, bees and butterflies in photographs of their natural **habitats**.

At the end of the book, there is information about the many ways birds help our food to grow. There is a list of new words and what they mean. Words you see in bold type are in this list. There is also a description of **pollination**. Bees, butterflies and some birds and other animals **pollinate** the plants of the world. They are called **pollinators**. Pollinators help many food crops and most of the wild plants in the world to grow. We need pollinators!

And birds, bees and butterflies are beautiful, too!

Aa

Anna's hummingbird

Anise swallowtail

Can you find Anna's hummingbird?

B b

Blue morpho

Bumble bee

Buckeye

Can you find the buckeye?

Cc

Checkerspot

Cedar waxwing

Cabbage white

D d

Dora's longwing

Ducks

Ee

Egret

F f

Field crescent

Can you find the field crescent?

G g

Glasswing

Golden-crowned sparrow

Gulf fritillary

H h

House finch

Hairstreak

Honey bee

Can you find the honey bee?

Ii

Isabella's longwing

Ibis

Jj

Jay

Kk

Kinglet

Kite

Kookaburra

Ll

Long-billed curlew

Lorquin's admiral

Lorikeet

Mm

Macaw

Monarch

Mylitta crescent

N n

Nuthatch

Night heron

Oo

Owl

Pp

Peacock

Phoebe

Postman

Q q

Quail

Rr

Robin

Red admiral

Red-legged honeycreeper

Ss

Stilt

Saddle-backed stork

Spotted towhee

Can you find the spotted towhee?

Tt

Thrush

Tiger swallowtail

Tanager

U u

Umber skipper

Vv

Violaceous euphonia

Ww

White-crowned sparrow

Woodpecker

Western bluebird

Can you find the woodpecker?

Xerces blue

This picture is of a butterfly collection in a museum because Xerces blue butterflies are extinct. That means they no longer exist in nature.

Yy

Yellow-rumped warbler

Yellowlegs

Can you find the yellow-rumped warbler?

Zz

Zebra longwing

Birds, Bees and Butterflies

Have you seen birds in your neighborhood? What did they look like?

Have you seen butterflies? Where? What color were they?

Have you seen any bees? What were they doing?

What are some things that are the same about birds and bees and butterflies?

Do they have wings? Can they fly? Do they like plants and flowers?

Something wonderful about birds, bees and butterflies is they help to grow our food. In fact, without birds, bees and butterflies, we would have a lot less food on Earth!

How Birds, Bees and Butterflies Help Our Food to Grow

Birds

Sowing Seeds

Some birds eat seeds and berries. As they fly from place to place, they drop seeds here and there while eating or pooping. The seeds fall onto the earth and some start to grow. Have you seen any birds eating seeds or berries? Finches, sparrows, robins and waxwings like to eat seeds and berries. Can you find any of those birds in this book?

Pollinating

Some birds drink **nectar**. Flowers make a sweet liquid called nectar. They also make a powder called **pollen**. When birds drink nectar, pollen gets on their beaks and feathers. When birds go to another flower, pollen on their bodies mixes with pollen in the new flower. This is called **pollination** and helps flowers to grow seeds. Hummingbirds, honeycreepers and lorikeets like to drink nectar. Can you find their pictures in this book?

Spreading Eggs

Some birds eat fish and creatures that live in water. These birds often have long legs and wade in shallow water, looking for food. As they wade, they spread fish eggs here and there which causes more fish to be born in more places in **marshes** and rivers. Egrets, herons, ibis, stilts and yellowlegs are wading birds. Can you find their pictures in this book?

Eating Bugs

Some birds eat bugs or small rodents like rats and gophers. This helps the balance of nature so that bugs and rodents don't eat all the plants. The kite eats small rodents. Phoebes, nuthatches, robins, bluebirds and sparrows eat insects. Can you find their pictures in this book?

Bees

Have you heard the saying "busy as a bee"? Bees are especially important to pollination. They buzz quickly from flower to flower, mixing the pollen that clings to their small bodies, and helping many plants to grow.

Butterflies

What about butterflies? They drink nectar. They flutter from flower to flower mixing the pollen dust that gets on their legs, wings and bodies when they drink. They are very important to pollination, helping plants to grow. How many butterflies do you see in this book? Are they drinking nectar?

New Words

Habitat

The place in nature where an animal or plant lives. A natural home.

Marsh

An area of soft, grassy land that is often covered by shallow water.

Nectar

A sugar water produced in flowers to attract insects and other animals.

Pollen

A fine powder produced in flowers. It is usually yellow.

Pollination

The moving of pollen to different parts of a flower, and from flower to flower. This causes plants to make seeds.

Pollinators

The insects and other animals which move pollen to different parts of a flower, and from flower to flower.

"Can you find them?" Answers

Anna's hummingbird

Field crescent

Buckeye

Honey bee

Spotted towhee

Woodpecker

Yellow-rumped warbler

Author's Note

When I was a child I loved to see birds flying high in the sky. I wondered, "Where do they live?" and "Where do they sleep at night?"

I decided to watch birds more closely. And when I do, I feel I am in another world. There are no words, and no talking, in this other world, but there is still a feeling of sharing. If I am patient, sometimes a bird sitting on a branch will turn and look at me. We watch each other quietly.

One day I saw a butterfly with its beautiful wings land on a flower. I decided to take its photograph. I began to study butterflies, too, and I learned they are pollinators and help plants to grow seeds. I began to watch all the butterflies in gardens and wild places. Sometimes if I sit very still, one might land close to me.

Watching these beautiful creatures, I feel how all life shares an unspoken universe. I have a wonderful feeling of belonging and freedom. It is the way I know we are all part of nature.

www.ingramcontent.com/pod-product-compliance
Lightning Source LLC
Chambersburg PA
CBHW041119300426
44112CB00002B/29